People who help us

Police Force

Jillian Powell

WAYLAND

Contents

1124980

All Wayland books encourage children to read and help them improve their literacy.

✓ The page numbers and index can be used to locate a particular piece of information.

✓ The glossary reinforces alphabetic knowledge and extends vocabulary.

✓ The books to read section suggests other books dealing with the same subject.

The Police Station

The police station is open night and day.

Police officers are based at the police station to answer **emergency calls**. There are **cells** for **suspects** and rooms where the officers **interview** people.

Police on Duty

There is always someone on duty at the enquiry desk.

People come into the police station if they have a problem, or to report a **crime**. The person on duty takes down the details so that a police officer can help.

The police sergeant talks to the officers at the start of the day.

The officers are told about what has happened on their **beat** and anything they should look out for while they are on **patrol.**

5

Community Police Officers

This police officer patrols on foot.

Community Police Officers get to know people in
their community so that they can help with any
problems or questions.

The police help when someone is lost or needs directions.

The police officer uses his two-way radio to report back to the station or to call for help.

Traffic Control

This police officer is on traffic duty.

The police help to keep the traffic moving when traffic lights are broken, or if there is a traffic jam. The officer uses an arm signal to show the drivers that they can go.

The police use speed cameras.

Speed cameras are set up by the road. They show how fast cars are travelling.

The police stop drivers who are going too fast.

The police officer's speed machine shows the driver has been speeding. She may have to pay a **fine** or go to **court** for breaking the speed limit.

Crowd Control

The police help to control big crowds.

At football matches, they stop people from running on to the pitch or fighting with fans from the other team.

Police officers keep crowds on the street under control.

This crowd has gathered to watch a royal procession. The police make sure that the people watching and taking part are safe.

Emergency Calls

Police officers in the control room answer emergency calls.

When someone rings the police, an officer in the control room puts all the details on to a computer. She sends out the nearest patrol car or motorcycle to help.

The officers in the patrol car hear a message from the control room.

The officers are told about a road accident. They can turn on a **siren** and a flashing blue light to warn other drivers that they are hurrying to an emergency call.

Road Accidents

The police use road signs to warn drivers that there has been an accident.

The police use road signs, traffic cones and flashing lights to warn other drivers to slow down or stop. They try to clear the road quickly and keep the traffic moving.

The police officer asks people how the accident happened.

The officer talks to the drivers and any **witnesses**, and writes down what they tell him. If people are injured, the police make sure they are taken to hospital in an ambulance.

Investigating Burglaries

Police officers find out about a house burglary.

The police officers talk to the house owner and any witnesses who may have seen the burglar. They note down what they have found out so that they can write a crime report.

These police officers are looking for fingerprints.

Detectives brush a special powder on to the doors and windows. If the burglar has left any fingerprints, the police can compare them with the fingerprints of any suspects.

Dog Handlers

Police dogs are trained to help find lost people.

A police dog works with its dog handler as a team.
Dog handlers train their dogs to use their sense of smell
to find people or things.

Police dogs can sniff out drugs.

The police use dogs to sniff out drugs in luggage at airports and stations. They check for bombs in public places such as shopping centres.

Mounted Police

Mounted police officers patrol on horseback.

Police horses must be carefully trained so that they are not afraid of traffic or big crowds.

These mounted police officers are outside a football ground.

Police horses are used at events where there are big crowds, such as festivals, sports events and **demonstrations.** Mounted police help to control crowds.

Helicopter patrols look for people who are lost or hiding.

The helicopter patrol officers in the air can see what is happening on the ground. They carry special equipment, such as cameras that help them to see in the dark.

Underwater teams search for missing people or things.

Underwater teams use boats. They are trained to dive underwater and search in rivers, lakes and canals.

Crime Prevention

Crime Prevention Officers help people to keep their homes safe.

They visit people and tell them how they can help to prevent a burglar from breaking in. The officers also visit shops and factories.

The police help people to set up Neighbourhood Watch schemes.

Neighbours can work together to help to prevent crime in their community. Crime Prevention Officers and **Special Constables** help them to keep their neighbourhood safe.

Police officers visit schools to talk about how to keep safe.

Community Police Officers talk to schoolchildren about problems such as bullying and drugs. They tell them how to stay safe by not talking to strangers or going alone to quiet places.

Police officers help children to learn about road safety.

The Community Police Officer teaches children the kerb drill so that they learn to cross busy roads safely.

Topic Web

ENGLISH
- Hold a 'Neighbourhood Watch' meeting
- Write a crime report

MATHS
- Make a chart of car crime statistics

SCIENCE
- Find out about fingerprints
- Draw from observation

INFORMATION TECHNOLOGY
- Use a database to compare burglary statistics
- Design Neighbourhood Watch posters and leaflets

HISTORY
- Find out about the history of the police
- Find out about the police uniform in history

Topic Web
POLICE FORCE

GEOGRAPHY
- Plan a route for a royal visit
- Map out a community beat

DESIGN AND TECHNOLOGY
- Design clothing for a 'bully patrol'
- Make a model of a house

ART
- Design fingerprint pictures
- Design string pictures and prints of fingerprints

MUSIC
- Write a rap about safety

P.E.
- Perform chase games

PERSONAL AND SOCIAL EDUCATION
- Make a personal safety plan

Notes for Teachers

Police work is central to the study of community and citizenship. Interpersonal skills can be developed through discussion and activities including group work and role play. Mathematical skills can be developed by applying statistics from the local area. Investigative and observational skills can be encouraged by creating imaginary situations requiring detective work through the use of clues.

Topics for Discussion

The work of the police force can lead to discussions on concepts of right and wrong, individual responsibilities to the community, crime and punishment. The need for rules and laws is central to a study of citizenship.

Police work links with personal safety issues such as drugs, bullying, and not talking to strangers.

Topic Web Activities

ENGLISH
• Speaking and listening   • Writing

Hold a Neighbourhood Watch meeting in your class to work out what could be done to make your neighbourhood safer (link with IT).

Imagine you are a detective investigating a burglary. Write a report about the crime, including a description of the stolen property, and interviews with the victim and a witness.

MATHS
• Using and applying maths   • Handling data

Find out some statistics for car crimes in your area. Make a chart to show the main facts, such as the number of cars stolen in a year, and the number of thefts from cars.

SCIENCE
• Life processes and living things (Humans as organisms)

• Experimental and Investigative Science

Find out about fingerprints and why they are used in police detective work. Make lists of other things which make us similar to and different from each other, and discuss which things we can change and which we can't. Using magnifying hand lenses, find out what type of fingerprint you have. Make a drawing from close observation.

I.T.
• Communicating and handling information

Find out the statistics for burglaries in your area over the past few years. Enter them into a database so that you can compare them.

On the computer, design posters and leaflets for a Neighbourhood Watch scheme for your neighbourhood (link with English).

HISTORY
• Historical enquiry   • Victorian Britain

Find out about the history of the police force, including the Bow Street Runners and the Metropolitan Police Force in London in Victorian times.

Find out what the police uniform was like in Victorian times and compare it with the modern uniform.

GEOGRAPHY
• Geographical skills

Use a town plan to work out the route for a royal visit. Find out the area of your local Community Police Officer's beat and plot it on a town plan.

D.T.
• Designing and making skills

Design items of clothing, such as printed T-shirts, arm bands and badges, for a 'bully patrol' in your school. Make badges and arm bands using your chosen logo. Make a model of a house and garden that a Crime Prevention Officer could use to talk about preventing house break-ins.

ART
• Investigating and making

Design and make fingerprint pictures, using fingerprints to paint crowd scenes or abstract images. Using drawings from observation (link with Science), make string pictures of fingerprints using string on black card. Paint the string so that you can make string prints of these fingerprints.

MUSIC
• Performing and composing

Write a rap about safety to warn children about danger and how to keep safe.

P.E.
• Games

Develop and perform chase games which involve running, chasing, dodging and avoiding.

PERSONAL AND SOCIAL EDUCATION
• Safety issues

As a class, make a list of your own rules for keeping safe.

Glossary

beat The area that a police officer patrols.

burglary Breaking into a building to steal things. A person who does this is called a burglar.

cell A small room, which is locked.

Community Police Officers Officers who help the people living in one area.

court A place where a judge decides how to punish people who have broken the law.

crime An act that breaks the law.

demonstrations Meetings where people gather or march to show how they feel about something.

detectives Police officers who look for clues to solve a crime.

fine A sum of money that a person is made to pay because he or she has broken the law.

interview A meeting where one person asks another person questions.

patrol To walk or drive round an area.

siren A loud horn or bell.

Special Constable A part-time police officer.

suspect Someone the police think has carried out a crime.

witnesses People who saw or heard what happened.

Books to Read

A Day in the Life of a Police Officer by Carol Watson
  (Franklin Watts, 1995)
Police Service by Philippa Perry and Stephen Gibbs
  (Wayland, 1994)
Police Station by Tim Wood (Franklin Watts, 1988)

Editors: Sarah Doughty and Cath Senker
Series editor: Sarah Doughty
Cover designer: Jan Sterling
Designer and typesetter: Malcolm Walker
Picture research: Shelley Noronha

First published in 1999 by
Wayland Publishers Ltd
61 Western Road, Hove
East Sussex, BN3 1JD

British Library Cataloguing in Publication Data
Powell, Jillian
  Police Force. – (People who help us)
  1. Police – Great Britain – Juvenile literature
  I. Title
363.2'0941

ISBN 0 7502 2252 2

Printed and bound by EuroGrafica, Vicenza, Italy

**Find Wayland on the Internet at
http://www.wayland.co.uk**

Index

Picture acknowledgements
Ace (Martin Bond) 15; Greg Evans International (Greg Evans) 20; Format (Judy Harrison) 26; Angela Hampton Family Life Pictures (Angela Hampton) 4, 7, 18, 25; Robert Harding 14; Impact (John Cole) 8, (Piers Cavendish) 9 (above), (John Cole) 12; Life File (David Kampfner) 13; Popperfoto 10; The Stockmarket 21, 27; Sylvia Cordaiy Photo Library (Elias Roston) 11; Topham (Press Association) 17 and 23, Wayland *title page*, Wayland (APM Studios) 3 and 5, (Tim Woodcock) 6, 9 (below), 16, 19, 22 and 24 (all APM). Cover pictures: Angela Hampton (main photo and top left); Photofusion/Paul Baldescare (top right); Wayland/APM (top middle).